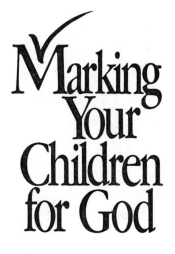

Marking
Your
Children
for God

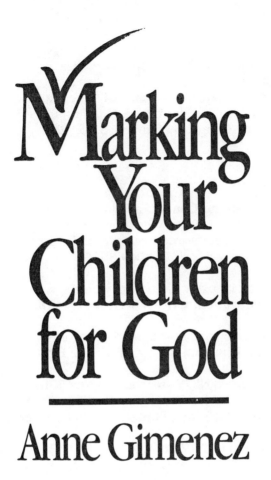

Marking Your Children for God

Anne Gimenez

Creation House
Altamonte Springs, Florida

Creation House
Strang Communications Company
190 N. Westmonte Drive
Altamonte Springs, FL 32714
(305) 869-5005

Unless otherwise noted, all Scripture references are
from the King James Version of the Bible.

Verses marked NKJV are from the New King James Version of the Bible. Copyright © 1979, 1980, 1982 by
Thomas Nelson Inc., Publishers. Used by permission.

Verses marked NIV are from the Holy Bible, New International Version. Copyright © 1973, 1978, 1984
by International Bible Society. Used by permission.

Quotations from "Television Show Finds Soviets Cannot Buy Religion" are reprinted from the Associated
Press. Used by permission.

First printing, December 1987
Second printing, March 1988

To my daughter, Robin Anne,
and all the young people of this generation
who are discovering what
it means to be marked for God.

Contents

ONE

How Good Is Your Aim?

Not long ago, I was speaking on a radio program about training our children to love and serve the Lord. In short, I stated that we as parents should encourage our children to make early commitments to the Lord. More than that, I believe children should not be allowed to wander aimlessly after that faith commitment because the Christian life, at any age, requires training and guidance.

Not more than a week later, I was amazed and deeply touched by a letter I received from a young woman, a college student who had heard the broadcast.

In it, she explained that she was the daughter of a minister. She had made a commitment to serve Christ when she was a little girl. But she had

11

rebelled from that as a teenager. Then she wrote something that caught my eye.

She admitted that her parents had been very liberal in the way they brought up their children. "My parents always allowed me to make my own decisions. I was allowed to decide whether or not I would go to church, and whether or not I would choose to serve God with my life. I was never made to live up to any kind of standard, and so for the last few years, I've gone my own way."

It was heartbreaking for me to think of her parents, a man and woman who apparently loved the Lord, as they had stood by watching while their daughter went the way of the world. But the young woman's conclusion was uplifting.

"After hearing what you had to say," she wrote, "I've renewed my childhood commitment to God, Anne. I'm going to live for Him and serve Him." She then asked for a copy of the broadcast, saying, "I have a teenage sister at home, and I'm going to send them this tape. I don't want them to raise her the way they raised me."

This young woman's letter brought to my mind the faces of countless men and women I have met from all across this country. So many, many times I have heard this question: "How can I raise my children so they will love and serve God?"

Then, in almost the same breath, I've heard these same Christian mothers and fathers say, "I know there is no guarantee when it comes to raising children. They all have to rebel, I guess. I just hope mine will come back to the Lord some day. After all, the Bible says, 'Train up a child in the way he should go, and when he is old he will not depart from it.' "

By this, I've understood them to mean that we should expect that our children may turn away from the faith. Then we should pray wistfully, hoping that just maybe the Bible is right and that they will serve the Lord once they come to their senses.

I must tell you that my husband, John, and I had to wrestle through our own questions about raising our daughter, Robin—who is not only a teenager but a preacher's kid to boot. Were we supposed to resign ourselves to the idea that Robin would turn away from the faith some day? That this was just *natural* and there was nothing we could do about it?

Faced with my own questions and concerns as a parent, I searched the Scriptures for answers. What I found stirred me greatly. In fact, it made me downright *angry*!

The first verse I turned to, as you might guess, was Proverbs 22:6. I examined it more closely:

Train up a child in the way he should go: and when he is old....

As I read, it occurred to me: Solomon is talking about faith for my child's *future*!

Suddenly, I saw a gaping hole in my faith as a parent. I, like so many others thought I was supposed to nurture my child carefully until she became a teenager. Then, just when she was hit with huge choices—about faith, her life-style, her friends and future—John and I were supposed to remove our hands. We were supposed to say, "Let's just let her rebel and hope that she gets it out of her system."

But that's the moment she would need us most, when she would face all the attractions of the world! How we had been brainwashed!

Since then, Robin has become a teenager. And I have seen that we, and thousands of other Christian parents, have been fooled into thinking that the soul of a teenager is sacrosanct. Worldly psychologists have painted a sign and hung it over the doorway to the teenage years, and it says, "No adults allowed."

Moreover, when young people hit that age when, abruptly, they want to sit in their room with the door closed, we parents lose our boldness. We knock meekly. We're afraid to ask too many questions. We hide in our prayer closets and pray desperately that they'll be able to resist the world's magnetism.

Basically, many Christian parents are scared to set down too many rules—maybe because we're afraid to have our authority challenged. That would be too crushing.

How did we get to be so fearful and fragile?

Friends, with all the evil that is bombarding our children we need to do more than grab onto one verse about *future-tense* faith! The signs of the times tell us that we are living in the last days. You see, for the last fifteen years or so, we've heard a lot of end-times teaching that tells us Jesus will return and whisk us out of this messed-up world. That would be nice.

But in the meantime, our children's destinies are at stake—and maybe their very lives.

We need a faith for them that is *present tense*. Why? Not just to keep them from falling away from the faith. As I have searched the Bible, I've been blessed and amazed to discover God's plan for your children and mine—a plan that was set in motion from the beginning. Why, He even spoke to Abraham about his children's children and their destinies.

God's Plan Revealed to Eve

God spoke first concerning the destinies of our children in Genesis. When He cursed the serpent, who was Lucifer in disguise, He also gave a promise to Eve:

> And I will put enmity between you and the woman, *and between your seed and her seed* (Gen. 3:15, NKJV, italics mine).

Obviously, this promise is a prophetic reference to Jesus Christ, who came to "crush" the serpent's head. Certainly, the Son of God crushed Satan's head. That is, Jesus regained from Satan his rule and evil government over the earth, which held us all in bondage to sin and death. But we are shortsighted if we let the verse go with that interpretation alone.

Listen to this! The apostle Paul assures us that we have "received the Spirit of sonship...We are God's children...heirs of God and co-heirs with Christ" (Rom. 8:15-17, NIV).

Do you understand what this means?

It's not just that we are adopted sons, receiving blessings from God. We and our children are co-heirs in destroying Satan's stranglehold on this earth. Abraham received the covenant promise of God along with his son Isaac and his grandson Jacob. They were heirs or inheritors together of the very same promises. Satan knows this divine destiny was invested in the seed of the woman. Not only through *the* Son of Man, but through the lives of every son and daughter of men, God plans to wound, bruise and ultimately annihilate Satan's government.

That's why Satan hates the entire human race and our children, our seed, in particular.

But if Satan has lost you and me to the body of Christ, he's desperate to devour our seed, our sons and daughters. Even literally. Just look at history as it's revealed in Scripture.

Warfare Against the Children

At strategic moments in history, we find that Satan has waged war, not only against adults who follow God, but against their offspring.

Exodus shows us one of those conflicts. Joseph had risen to power in Egypt, and his whole family found safety there during a terrible famine. But when Joseph died, "a new king, who did not know about Joseph, came to power" (Ex. 1:8, NIV). He made the Hebrews slaves, but they kept multiplying. Soon, by some estimates, they were several million strong.

What did this new king do?

First, he ordered the midwives to kill every boy-child as it came from its mother's womb. When the women refused, he gave a more hideous decree: Every infant son was to be thrown into the Nile!

We can imagine the horror and wailing as the Hebrew parents watched helplessly as the king's soldiers flung their babies into the river to drown or be eaten by crocodiles.

One Levite family had a plan, however. They hid their newborn in a basket. This son, of course, was Moses. He survived the king's rage and eventually led the Hebrews out of Egypt's bondage and to the borders of the promised land where they became God's own nation.

Centuries later, Israel's wicked King Herod was visited by wise men from the East. When Herod asked them where they were going, they answered and said they were following a star that foretold the coming of a child of divine destiny.

Herod's response was to order that every male child under two years of age be slaughtered. But that did not prevent Jesus from growing up, giving His life on the cross of Calvary and ushering in God's church. That is, He opened the way for everyone in the whole earth to become an "heir" of God, as Paul said later.

Now step back from these two historic scenes for a moment. Look behind the events. We see two strategic moments in spiritual history. In the first, God wanted to father a godly nation—Israel. In the second, He wanted to father a church from every kindred, tongue and tribe in the whole world. And both times, Satan raged and brought destruction upon little children.

Is this ringing a bell? Does it make you think about the incredible wave of drugs and alcohol addiction that is sweeping our young people? Or the epidemic of teenage suicide? What about the unborn—some *three million* in the United States alone at the time of this writing—who are aborted, torn limb from limb, or burned with saline injections in their mothers' wombs?

My point is this: If Satan tried to block God's plan for bringing forth a godly nation and a worldwide, multicultural church by attacking the children, what does he see coming now? Why is the spirit of murder loose in our world today to such a degree? What is he trying so furiously to stop?

To put it another way: God is unveiling a powerful plan right now for our sons and daughters, in this very hour. And we as Christian parents must not sit idly by, adopting the hands-off attitude of the world, and allow them to be snatched away from their godly heritage.

We *can* shape our children and help prepare them to take part in God's great plan. God doesn't mean for you and your children to fight each other—He wants you to get ready to go to war *together*!

How? Listen to this call to godly parents from the Psalms:

> Lo, children are an heritage of the Lord: and the fruit of the womb is His reward. As arrows are in the hands of a mighty man; so are the children of the youth. Happy is the man that hath his quiver full of them: they shall not be ashamed, but they shall speak with the enemies in the gate (Ps. 127:3-5).

Our children are meant to be a blessing, a reward, not a curse. But that requires our involvement. Look closely at the passage. We are to consider our children "as arrows in the hands of a mighty man."

What does that mean?

The Arrows in Your Hand

First of all, arrows don't grow on trees—green branches do. To fashion an arrow requires work. If you were a warrior at the time this psalm was written, you would go out and find the straightest twig possible, cut it off the tree, then go about drying and shaping it. You would smooth the rough or crooked parts. You would apply a little pressure to be sure there were no weak spots. You would take time and great care yourself to make each arrow—because your life could well depend on their flying straight and true.

When it comes to fashioning our "arrows" this passage says to me, "Don't allow the world to warp your children. Lay hands on them. Polish and scrape them if necessary." I don't want someone else making my arrow for me. I'll make it myself, thank you. My life, or hers, may depend upon it.

Second, you not only shape an arrow, you fit it into a bow and aim it. You direct it at a target.

Third, with all your might you draw back your bow and let the arrow fly—right to its mark.

Nothing in this description of shaping and shooting an arrow sounds like the hands-off approach some have been duped into accepting. I see that I must use skill, craftsmanship. I must know the target. I must put all my might into this effort. Solomon said, "Whatever your hand finds to do, do it with all your might" (Eccl. 9:10, NIV).

Can we apply this to our careers or ministries and not to the rearing of our children? Can we invest in homes, cars, hobbies—even good Christian activities—and neglect the spiritual shaping of our special inheritance?

I learned something else recently about making arrows. When some of the American Indians made arrows, they added one more step to the process. Each man would add a special small design or mark to his arrow. Then, if he was hunting with a party of other men and they all let fly at once, each man could easily retrieve his arrow. How? He could tell it from the others because it bore his own special mark.

Marking Your Children for God

Friends, we have a great calling and privilege as Christian parents. We can mark our children for God.

When the Holy Spirit first revealed this truth to me, I was full of questions.

What does God require of my own life?

What goals am I aiming at? Am I walking in step with God's plan or shooting at my own mark?

How do I become a godly parent? How do I discipline in a godly way?

I have had to face these questions as a Christian parent. And I've had to search out the answers in Scripture. It has been a challenging and surprising journey for my family—John, Robin and me— as we have learned how to grow in faith *together*.

We are discovering now, day by day, the joy of being a godly family. My prayer for you, as you read this book, is that you will pick up the trail, too!

As godly parents, struggling and winning in one of the greatest battles of all time, you will find yourself in good company. It was in the lives of great men and women of the faith—like Abraham and Hannah, the mother of Samuel—that I found inspiration to be stronger as a Christian parent.

It's from these fathers and mothers in the faith that we will find our first insights in the joyous task of marking *our* children for God.

TWO

Faith of Our Fathers— And Our Mothers, Too

*S*omething has gone wrong with our society. Ministers shake their heads at the massive number of Christians who pop in and out of a congregation like grasshoppers the moment the pastor's sermons don't make them happy. We hear about the high rate of divorce and say, "People just don't have any sense of commitment."

Is lack of commitment really the problem? Yes, on one level. But I believe there is a deeper problem.

It's not just that we are living in the "me-first-second-and last" generation. Many of us have no vision for ourselves and God's plan for our future, let alone for our children. When we read in Psalms that "children are an heritage from the Lord," we aren't too impressed because we don't have a clue as to what "heritage" really means.

I believe that the first step you need to take, if you want to mark your children for God, is to restore your vision of God's plan for your family.

A Godly Inheritance

Throughout the Bible we find that God made no secret of His desire, not just for godly individuals, but for whole families as well. Often, when He called a man or woman to Himself, He also showed them a glimpse of His plan for their sons and daughters—even their grandchildren!

Abraham, who is known as the father of faith, was called out of an idol-worshipping land. Immediately, God showed him a divine destiny:

> The Lord had said to Abram..."I will make you into a great nation and I will bless you...all peoples on earth will be blessed through you...Look up at the heavens and count the stars—if indeed you can count them...So shall your offspring be...kings will come from you (Gen. 12:1-3; 15:5; 17:6, NIV).

From Abraham issued the patriarchs Isaac and Jacob, known as Israel. From Israel came the twelve tribes, the priests of God, King David, King Solomon and all the prophets. And eventually, through the body of a humble young woman named Mary came Jesus, Son of God and Savior of the world. Can you imagine—all of this passing by your eyes in a split second?

From the moment that God revealed His plan to Abraham, every boy and girl who was to come from His seed was a *marked* child. If you were a Hebrew child, you knew it.

Consider the story of Moses. His parents had wrapped him and set him floating in the Nile in a basket of reeds to save him from Pharaoh's death sentence. When the daughter of Pharaoh found the basket, she drew it up out of the water, unwrapped the baby from his little blanket and said, "It's one of the Hebrew children." How did she know that?

Because Abraham took seriously the covenant he'd made with God and followed His instruction that every male child was to be circumcised on the eighth day of his life. He had taught this covenant to his sons and daughters, who also implanted the covenant in the minds of *their* sons and daughters. On and on it went for generations. Pharaoh's daughter knew she was holding a child who was marked for God.

Now this covenant left more than a physical marking on Moses. It marked his mind and heart, too. When he became a man, he saw that his people's situation in Egypt just didn't square with what his great-great-great-granddaddy Abraham had said God had in mind for the Hebrews. They were supposed to be a great nation, blessing all the earth, and here they were toiling as slaves.

Moses knew the promises, and he knew things

had to be made right. Unfortunately, he tried to take matters into his own hands at first. But later, when God got ahold of him, he was molded into a great leader and lawgiver. In fact, the laws that God imparted to Moses shaped the legal justice system under which we operate today.

So the vision that God gave to Abraham, that of a free nation of godly people, came down through generations and fired the spirit of Moses. And so God's promise was fulfilled.

Investing in Your Children

How do we today catch hold of God's promises and vision for our families? How do we mark our children, investing in them the sense of divine destiny?

First, you can lay hold of the truths in God's Word concerning your household. Let me remind you of a few:

The fruit of your womb will be blessed...The Lord will grant...abundant prosperity [to your children] (Deut. 28:4,11, NIV).

How good and pleasant it is when brothers live together in unity (Ps. 133:1, NIV).

Believe in the Lord Jesus, and you will be saved—you and your household (Acts 16:31, NIV).

Do you begin to catch the vision for what the Lord has in mind for your family? Health and abundant prosperity, peace and unity. Eternal life with Him. The problem for some of us is that we can believe God for ourselves—we can even believe Him for a house, a job or a new car if we need one. But we have a hard time trusting Him to reach our sons and daughters.

"Sure," you may object, "but my children have a will of their own."

What child doesn't have a will of his own? They're all born with it.

Children whose hearts are set toward God are rare, in my experience. This is where God wants to involve you in the marking process. We can lay the foundations of a godly inheritance in two ways: by *commitment* and by *example*.

Commitment

Let's look at Abraham again. In Genesis 18:19, God said of him,

> For I have known him [Abraham], that he may *command* his children and his household after him, that they keep the way of the Lord to do righteousness and justice... (NKJV, italics mine).

Some parents are afraid to command their children. Not Abraham. Many parents today have been confused by worldly influences—and some other-worldly ones too—and they are thinking it isn't godly to be strong with their children. We must never be afraid to say or do or insist upon what is right. I can't imagine Abraham saying to Isaac, "We're going to Hebron to worship God. Would you like to come with us, or would you like to stay home and play with the sheep?"

That, however, is the kind of choice some parents offer their children. When it comes to church or Sunday school, they say, "I don't want to force my faith on little Johnny." But then little Johnny comes home and declares, "I'm joining the school baseball team"—which means you'll have to delay dinner four nights a week while he's at practice and you'll have to give up the next sixteen Saturdays to be at his games. And we don't question *that* kind of decision at all—unless it's to ask Johnny if he'd like to have a new baseball glove.

Now I know this sounds strong, but many of us, even Christian parents, are weak when it comes to involving our children in the things of God. We're fearful, when we should be saying, "Son, this family goes to church. This family prays and reads the Bible together. You're in this family and that's what you do."

Hannah, the mother of the prophet Samuel, obviously had no trouble shaping her son's will and the direction of his life. We know that, although Hannah was apparently barren, she came to God at Shiloh and made this covenant with Him:

O Lord Almighty, if you will only look upon your servant's misery...and not forget your servant but give her a son, then I will give him to the Lord for all the days of his life (1 Sam. 1:11, NIV).

God honored her faith, and soon after, Hannah gave birth to a son whom she named Samuel.

Now Samuel was still a very little boy—the Bible says he was weaned—when Hannah fulfilled her vow to God. She took him back to Shiloh and presented him to Eli the priest. Note this: *As yet, Samuel had no knowledge of God for himself.*

Nevertheless, his mother had dedicated him into the Lord's service. She had talked to him, saying, "You will serve God because I made a commitment, not because you made one. You are God's man, and His temple will be your home." She trained him and followed through on her part. Now it was up to God to fulfill His end.

A little further we read:

> The boy Samuel ministered to the Lord before Eli *[that is, he carried out simple temple duties]*...Now Samuel did not yet know the Lord: The word of the Lord had not yet been revealed to him (1 Sam. 3:1,7, NIV, italics added).

Then "the Lord called Samuel" (verse 4). And when He came to Samuel, the boy's heart was prepared to receive Him. Certainly, every child must come to his own personal relationship with God in Jesus Christ. For as Jesus said, "No one comes to the Father except through me" (John 14:6, NIV). But we, like Hannah, can still live a

29

life of steadfast commitment before God. Then, when the Lord calls to our children, their hearts will be ready and open. Like Samuel, they will be inclined to have that initial openness to His Spirit, and say, "Speak, Lord, Your servant is listening."

Example

A distinction needs to be made between commitment and example. Some people are great on commitment—at least on the surface. They're in church every time the doors open. They're at every Bible study. That's all well and good.

But all of us parents need to take a long hard look at the kind of example we are setting for our children at home, Monday through Saturday.

Let me give you two illustrations.

There used to be a commercial on television that showed a father walking along a path with his son, a cute little blond-headed boy. Everything the father did, the son imitated. The father picked up a stone and skipped it on a pond—the boy tried to do the same. The father sat down with his back to a tree—the boy propped himself at his daddy's side. The father lit up a cigarette....Well, I think you get the point. The final picture was of the cute child looking thoughtfully at his daddy.

Our children watch us like hawks. They pick up on our smallest gestures and expressions.

Once, when Robin was still a baby, a friend was visiting in our home. While we were chatting, I glanced over at Robin to see if she was playing safely, and she made the strangest, wrinkled-up face at me. It occurred to me that she did this a lot, but this was the first time it had happened with anyone else around.

Since I was a new mother, I asked my friend, "Did you see that? Is there something wrong—is she feeling some kind of pain when she makes that face?"

My friend started to chuckle. "Anne, every time you talk to her, you wrinkle up your nose and smile right into her face. She's only doing it back to you!"

We both got a good laugh. But it made me think twice about the things in me I wanted my daughter to imitate. It's made me think many times about the ways I influence her without even knowing it.

Now I don't want to be hard on anyone, but I need to ask a few tough questions:

When you get mad at your preacher, or if his sermon is too long on Sunday, what do you say about him in front of your children? Do you bless him—or bless him out?

When you have to pay your tithe, or your taxes, do your children hear you grumbling and complaining, or do you bless God and thank Him for the government He's placed over you?

If your boss gives you a hard time, do you tell your kids what a no-good so-and-so the man is? Or do you ask your children to pray with you that God will change his heart?

When money is tight and bills are piling up, do

you panic and tear your hair, or do you pray and ask God to give you (along with the needed finances) the gift of a peaceful, trusting heart?

I think you see what I'm getting at. We can mark our children's hearts, not only in *negative* ways, but also in *positive* ways!

Friends, while we're praying for our children, we need to let Him make us the beautiful vessels of His Spirit that He wants us to be. We need to ask Him to straighten us out, clean us up and polish us. This is God's will as revealed in the Bible.

Peter wrote that Christ was an example to us of purity, holiness, faithfulness, honesty and even suffering (1 Pet. 2:21-23).

Likewise, in 2 Thessalonians 3:9 Paul said, "We...make ourselves an example of how you should follow us" (NKJV).

In another passage he tells Timothy, "Be an example to the believers in word, in conduct, in love, in spirit, in faith, in purity" (1 Tim. 4:12, NKJV).

Paul also warned the Corinthians, a church that was a very poor example of Christ-likeness, not to get so caught up in spiritual gifts. (Some of us today still have a tendency to do that.) Instead, he told them to let love be their highest aim, because it is the "more excellent way" (1 Cor. 12:31).

Why is love so important—more important even than spiritual gifts?

Because love represents all the fruit of the Spirit, which reveal the character of Christ. Character is what lasts.

Character is also what children are so good at reading. Up to a certain age, parents are the biggest, most important people in the eyes of each child. These younger years are the time to plant in a child's character the need to be committed to God and His church. And it's a time to demonstrate to them that God wants to and can *live and move through each human being*.

This is crucial because, after that age of innocence, come the teenage years, a time of questioning, weighing and deciding. If our children have been marked *in their spirits* by the impact of a godly parent—that is, one who seeks to let the character of God rule—they will be more inclined to say, "There really was something different about Mom and Dad. They lived up to what they believed. I guess this stuff about God is true."

Let me tell you plainly, from my heart: You can have all the gifts of the Spirit, but if you don't have the godly character to match, your gifts are as sounding brass and a tinkling cymbal (especially to your children!).

On the other hand, I believe the Bible shows me that when I live out the characteristics of Jesus in my life—love, joy, peace, patience, kindness, goodness, meekness, gentleness, self-control—that the world and our children can have no argument against us. In fact, I believe that the character traits in my life will rub off my child at a very basic and true level.

So the need for *commitment* and *example* stand before us then. Not to browbeat, condemn or shame us. But to challenge, encourage and give us great hope! We can get involved in Christian good works. We can pray for and see miracles of power. We hope these things will witness to our children, and they do.

But nothing has so much impact as the quiet, strong character of Jesus lived out in our daily lives.

Let your life be clean and true before God, and it will be the first sharp tool God uses in marking your child for Him.

THREE

Slaying the Giants

As we saw in the previous chapter, the lives of the Old Testament patriarchs were examples of commitment that we can learn from. They were not only willing to commit themselves to God, but they were willing to commit the lives of their children to Him, too.

Now I know that looking at the lives of these great heroes of the faith and great saints can make you feel that maybe you can't measure up. One person said to me, "The problem with saints is that they're so saintly. They always do everything right!"

My purpose, however, is to encourage you, not make you feel bad. After all, if you've got to model someone, you might as well strive to model the best!

Still, we know that the men and women of the Old Testament were far from perfect. All the time God was trying to shape them into a godly nation and place them in the land He had for them, they had to fight many battles—not only against physical forces, but against their own wavering faith and inability to do things God's way.

God wanted to give them a beautiful inheritance—a special land and children with godly hearts—and they had a rough time laying hold of His promises. Now I can identify with *that* struggle, can't you?

When we have begun to lay hold of God's promise that He will give us a godly inheritance in our children, there are major spiritual battles to be fought. I want to examine an important Scripture passage that will reveal how those battles can be won.

Recently, the Lord spoke to my heart, directing me to Deuteronomy 2. That chapter describes the end of Israel's wilderness wanderings. There I read:

> And the space in which we came from Kadesh-barnea [the place where they crossed into the wilderness], until we were come over the brook Zered [into Canaan], was thirty and eight years (v. 14).

I believe we are in an important period in history. In May 1948, when Israel became a nation, I believe the church of Jesus Christ began to head toward a crucial "crossing-over" point. Now, decades later, we are starting to enter into an inheritance.

In a later chapter, we're going to examine the urgent significance of where we, as a church, stand at this moment. But for now, let's continue to focus on the warfare we must wage for the future of our children.

What I found in this passage is crucial in fighting the fight of faith.

Moses wrote the early part of Deuteronomy, I discovered, on the first day of the last month of that fortieth year as he reminisced over all the wanderings. He reveals that the distance between Kadesh-barnea and Canaan was only an eleven-day journey—a mere 160 miles, according to one commentary. Can you imagine, an eleven-day journey that took forty years!

But of course distance had nothing to do with it. Mileage was not the issue. They knew exactly where Canaan was and where the crossing-over point would be, and they could have headed toward it at any time. Yet we know so well that their disobedience caused the Lord to turn them away right at the border, and they wandered.

At the end of that time, Moses records:

All the generation of the men of war were wasted from among the host (Deut. 2:14).

In other words, all those who had a problem with entering into the life of the Spirit of God had to be taken out from among the people.

Now there are people even today who are uncomfortable with entering into what the Lord is doing. So many of us are tempted to "circle the wagons" and settle down right where we are. No amount of Holy-Spirit nudging will budge us at times.

Imagine the mark it can leave on a child's spirit when he's taken to church and he hears that our God is the God of miracles. But then, when a crisis comes up at home, he sees his parents in complete panic. And think of the impact it makes when a child hears that God is holy, but at home the standards are unclear.

Even worse, sometimes we make God out to be the "nice, old grandpa upstairs" who pats us on the head when we sin and says, "That's OK."

That says to a child, "My parents' faith isn't real. Maybe God isn't powerful enough to do all those things He promises in the Bible. Maybe it doesn't matter whether I obey God's Word. Come to think of it, maybe the Bible isn't true at all."

Reading about the generation that had to die in the wilderness, I whispered a heartfelt prayer that God would always keep *my* spirit open to His promptings. Who wants to go 'round and 'round in a desert? And who wants their children to conclude, by seeing their parents' lack of faith, that the Bible is just a nice storybook, not to be trusted as true?

Focusing back on the Scriptures, I saw that, at

the end of those years in the wilderness, some-thing unusual happened. In Deuteronomy 2:24, the Lord told the people,

Rise ye up, take your journey, and pass over the river Arnon:...begin to possess [the land].

Before they could possess it, however, the Israelites had to contend with two kings who stood in their way. Not only were they powerful, but in Numbers 13, where the story is told in detail, they are identified as giants.

Now I believe that these two kings represent something spiritually—two giant obstacles that would keep us from heading into the wonderful inheritance God has promised for us and our families. And every one of us must come to our own Kadesh-barnea, our own place of crossing over from wandering spiritually to possessing the land. How do we do that?

First of all, even before we face the giants in the land, we have to decide that we're not satisfied with the blessings of the wilderness.

You say, "Now hold on a minute. Blessings of the wilderness? What are you talking about?"

If you really look at Scripture, the wilderness was full of blessings! The Israelites knew the leading of God's Spirit. They were protected from the scorching sun by a cloud, and they were led at night by a pillar of fire. They had meat to eat, water from a rock. Their shoes never wore out. All that was in the wilderness.

Likewise, you can take stock of all the daily blessings—a nice home, reasonably good children—and get to thinking that you're in the promised land. Maybe you are—and maybe you're not. I tell you this not to discourage you but to let you know for a certainty that God always has *more*!

But what were the "giants," and what do they represent to us today as Christian parents? If you don't know your enemy, you'll never slay him.

In Numbers 13 we hear the Israelites exclaiming, "We can't go into Canaan. Those people are big—and we are like grasshoppers compared to them!" (See vv. 31,33.)

The first giant was fear. Yes, the Bible tells us the first king they faced was Sihon, king of the Amorites. But what he instilled in their hearts was terror.

What kind of fear are we talking about today?

The first thing Christian parents fear is that their children will hate or ignore Jesus Christ. Their fear becomes like an infection. Soon they are almost transmitting to their children the unspoken message, "I *know* you're going to rebel and turn away from the Lord."

This kind of fear is a special challenge for a Christian man or woman whose spouse is not a Christian, and for those who are divorced and whose former spouse is living an ungodly lifestyle. I have talked to so many whose hearts ache because they are struggling to be good Christians, to involve their children in church and Christian youth groups—only to feel that all their hard work and prayers are being undone by the unbelieving parent. They agonize, doubting the effectiveness of their attempts to train their children properly.

How often my heart has gone out to the women who have said, "My kids were doing fine until they had to visit my ex-husband. He's such a bad influence."

If you are afraid that your children are being negatively influenced by your husband or wife who is not a believer, I have great news for you—and it is straight from the Word of God.

The apostle Paul says,

For the unbelieving husband is sanctified by the wife, and the unbelieving wife is sanctified by the husband; otherwise your children would be unclean, but now they are holy (1 Cor. 7:14, NKJV).

The word "holy" means complete, entire, sound, set apart for sacred use. It is too easy to focus on the negative influences on our children and shrink in fear. Regardless of what circumstances we find ourselves in, none of us need ever stop telling our children that they *are* set aside for God's use. Tell them they are God's creation, that His hand is on them and that they have a call on their lives. Tell them they are the hope of future generations, and perhaps they shall literally see the second coming of our Lord.

We can never allow our *sight* to overcome

our *faith*.

There is a second kind of fear, which I believe most parents have to deal with regarding their children.

Jesus said, "If you lose your life, you'll find it."

Paul said, "I die daily. My life is on the line for God all the time." Shipwrecked, beaten and left for dead, his only real fear was that he would stop fighting the battle!

Friends, have you stopped waging the fight of faith? Are you allowing the world to dictate to you what standards will rule your home? Have you allowed a fear of "offending" your neighbors, a fear of not fitting in, to steal your witness for Christ?

Have you been afraid that, if your children are led along a godly path, their friends will laugh at them?

I know so well that none of us wants our child to be laughed at. How painful it is for a parent when a child comes home from school and says, "The other kids laugh at me. No one likes me."

Believe me, I know that no parent wants his child to be the "oddball." If you want to lead your family in godliness, you're going to have to slay the giant of "the fear of men." If we fear men, we will have little respect for God and His desires for us.

But wait—! I'm also talking about something more than a fear of "what the neighbors will think."

Hebrews says there are people who, all their lives, are subject to bondage because of the fear of death (Heb. 2:15). Death. What does that mean—just losing my physical life? No. Death, in the New Testament sense, means losing my ambitions, my money, my house, my rung on the career ladder, my friends, *myself*.

And it can mean giving up *my* dreams for my child in order to let God place a high calling in his heart.

Some folks will say, "Wait a minute. There's nothing wrong with wanting my child to be a doctor." That's true. I'm not saying that every son or daughter has to be a missionary or they aren't in the service of the Lord. I *am* saying that, as parents, it is entirely natural for us to want to fulfill our dreams through the lives of our children.

Let me ask. Are you afraid to place your children squarely in the hands of God?

God's word to you is, "Fear not!"

Now what is the second giant? It's very subtle. In Deuteronomy 1:26, when Moses was reminiscing over the beginning of the conquest of Canaan, he says,

> You *would not* go up [into Canaan], but *rebelled* against the command of the Lord your God (NKJV, italics mine).

Rebellion is the second giant. How does rebellion show its head? Murmuring. Complaining. Unwillingness to enter into the life of the church.

Do you complain about the pastor and his sermons in front of your children? Do you knock your elders and deacons? Do you poke fun at the dresses the pastor's wife wears or the way she styles her hair?

Those are the petty things. How about these? When you disagree with your pastor, or when you just get a little lazy, do you make an excuse to absent yourself from church?

What you are saying to your children is, "A little rebellion doesn't hurt. Rebellion doesn't matter to God."

Rebellion does matter! It is the other giant that will keep you from entering the promises God has for your family.

This is hard, friends, but I must say it. Too many times we blame God when our children are cold toward the faith. But children can catch our attitudes!

There is a story of a little boy who said to his mother, "I don't want to go to church anymore."

Startled and upset, the mother said, "Why is that?"

The boy replied, "I don't think church is important."

She was shocked. "How could you say such a thing?"

"Because when I go to the movies," he responded, "you give me five dollars. But when I go to church, you only give me twenty-five cents for the offering."

Suddenly, she saw—as clearly as her son saw—just how much she valued church. I should say, how little.

Parents, the last thing I want is for you to feel condemned. I am not trying to set up some high standard of "godliness" that is unrealistic and unattainable.

But I do want you to come away with *conviction*!

Time and again, I've heard Christian parents bemoan when a child is in rebellion. Time and again, when a child is caught drinking alcohol or smoking or looking at dirty magazines, I've heard parents say, "How can I tell them it's wrong when I do it myself?"

There is good news! You can turn the situation around. Once we've identified the giants of ungodly fear and rebellion in ourselves we can conquer them! Ask the Holy Spirit right this minute to reveal any fearful or rebellious ways in you.

Rebellion is not something to fool around with. When you find encampments of it in your life, ask God to put His sword to it. Ask Him to wipe it out!

In the book of Numbers we see how God dealt with the rebellious kings and people of Canaan who worshipped idols and demon gods. He said, "Wipe out the men, women, children—even the cattle." To us in the conservative, "enlightened" twentieth century that sounds brutal. But when you're talking about rebellion, His Word is still the same. "Don't tolerate it for a minute. Clean it out!"

Mothers, fathers, I believe that "he which hath begun a good work in you will perform it" [that is, work until it is complete] (Phil. 1:6). Can you accept that? Can you recommit yourself to that truth in the areas of your life where it applies?

When we've opened ourselves to His new, deeper work, we can live honestly and in peace before our children, free of guilt. Then we're no longer just parents; we become parents in the Lord.

Once we wage those battles, we gain a spiritual ground, an authority in our homes. And that makes possible a new relationship with our children in which we can shape them with confidence for God.

Yes, though you may have been clinging to certain areas of your life or harboring attitudes of rebellion, that can change today. Why not ask God to do some "house cleaning"?

Now, having faced the "giants," let's go on to look at the shaping and marking of our children that can take place when we learn how to parent them in the Lord!

FOUR

A Parent in the Lord

*T*his charge I commit to you, son Timothy, according to the prophecies previously made concerning you, that by them you may wage the good warfare, having faith and a good conscience... (1 Tim. 1:18,19, NKJV).

In Paul's first and second letters to Timothy, the apostle writes to the young leader as his "son in the faith." Certainly, we can learn from the love and concern Paul showed for this young man who was not even his flesh-and-blood son. But more important than that, I believe we need to see our own children as Paul saw Timothy—as *children in the Lord*.

So many of us get caught up in the everyday goals we set for our children. First, the young parents' goal is simply to get their child out of diapers and into pre-school. Then we center on good grades, reasonably good behavior and piano or dance or swimming lessons. Then it's getting them into and out of braces, through high school and into a good college. We are all so taken up with the practical things of life.

However, I believe no natural goal is the right goal to set for our children. Graduating from Harvard or Princeton with a Ph.D.—though not a bad thing in itself—is not what we, as Christian parents, should set our sights on. We are to set our hearts and the hearts of our children on "the prize of the high calling of God in Christ Jesus" (Phil. 3:14).

What? Isn't that putting too much pressure on little Johnny or Suzie? Won't that turn them off to God completely? *Pressure* will indeed turn off a child to the things of God. It offends most adults, too. But we're not talking about pressure.

Don't we, as Americans, tell our children: "This is a wonderful country, a place where you can grow up to be anything you want to be"? Well, why don't we just turn things around and allow that same hearty mindset to invade our faith? Let's start telling our children: "We live in a wonderful kingdom—the kingdom of God—and in this kingdom, God may call you to be anything!"

One of the reasons we don't take this approach, I believe, is that we often go at parenting from a purely natural viewpoint. Whether we like to admit it or not, most of us are still reacting to the way our parents brought us up. How often do you say, "I'll never let my kids get away with the things I was allowed to do." Or "My folks *made* me do such-and-such, and I'll never force my child to do that." We spend so much time trying to counter the past that we can hardly enjoy the present, let alone prepare for the future.

God as Our Parent

One sure way to break out of this reactionary mode and become the right kind of parent is to refocus our attention on God. Since He is the eternal Father of all, He can teach us how to parent.

Let's examine, first of all, some of the many ways in which God parents us, His children.

God is quick to forgive. When I sincerely repent—that is, turn away from—wrongdoing, my heavenly Father always forgives. Likewise, when your child has sinned or disobeyed, you must learn to forgive quickly.

Practically speaking, this means that we do not store up offenses but deal with them quickly. It means learning to overlook some childish mistakes even when they are made time and time again. For instance, it is not a forgiving attitude to say to your five-year-old who accidentally knocks over his milk, "You're the clumsiest kid I know. You *always* spill your milk."

This kind of labeling says to a child that you have not forgotten or forgiven the last time he spilled his milk. It leaves in his mind the question, "Am I really forgiven now?"

If you say, "I forgive you"—and I recommend that you do verbalize forgiveness—then let it mean that the offense will not be brought up again later.

God loves me unconditionally. Never make your love conditional. Your general approval of your child as a person cannot depend on whether he has gotten good grades or behaves well.

In this, we must learn as parents to distinguish between the child and his offense. We often say, as Christians, "Hate the sin, not the sinner." But maybe we betray the real, conditional love that's in our heart when our child does something and we forget to make the same distinction.

We can and must learn this unconditional love, because it is the most powerful motivating factor in a child's life.

God never forsakes me. I have never been forsaken by God when I was in trouble. At times we may think, in our unbelieving way, that He has deserted us, but that is not the truth.

Christian parents need to make a distinction between encouraging a child to do things on his own—which builds self-confidence—and turning him away when he is in need or in trouble. Being there for your child gives substance to your religion. This leads to the next point.

God never lets me down. My heavenly Father never disappoints me. I know that His Word and His promises are true.

This says to me that I should make good on my promises. If I have promised my child that I will attend a school or sports function or will do something special for them on a certain day, then I should do it.

So many times I've heard young people say, "My mom always promised to take me to such-and-such a place, but when the time came she was too busy." Or "My dad works all the time. He never comes to any of my games."

Now there are times when we just cannot make good on a promise for legitimate reasons. Surprise business trips come up. Finances get a bit tight. When these happen, however, we should not just break the promise and shrug it off. It's a simple thing to learn to say, "I'm sorry; we just can't do it this time." You may also wish to explain why there is a problem, even if the child is too young to understand fully.

The next thing to do is *reschedule* the missed event. This lets your child know that being with him and living up to your word is important. Even if he doesn't make a big deal out of a disappointment, underneath it is important to him.

When He says no, it's for my own good. I can whine, pout and run around to Christian counselors to try to get another answer—but I've found that once God says no, He sticks with it. Isn't it wonderful to know that He has that kind of stability? It makes His yes so much more meaningful!

When we are wishy-washy with our children

it leaves them confused. It gives them grounds to ask, "Did God really say, 'Thou shalt not...?' " Does that question sound familiar?

Many of us have the tendency to change our decisions the moment our children whine. I can excuse myself by saying, "I'm just soft-hearted," or "I don't think a parent should be so strict." But the real truth, most of the time, is that we don't want to face the hassle and the complaining!

We need to search God's Word, pray about how to apply His standards to our specific situation—then stand firm by our decision.

God is always there when I need Him. Catherine Marshall, in her book *Meeting God at Every Turn*, has a chapter called "Our Father, Who Art on Earth." In it, she recalls that her father, who was a busy preacher, always allowed her to come into his study, no matter how pressing the thing he was involved in. She would quietly come and stand at his desk, and he would quickly finish up his work for the moment. Then he would say, "Yes, Catherine, what is it?" From that moment, she had his full attention for as long as she needed him.

To live with children is to be interrupted. We can certainly teach our children not to interrupt rudely when we are talking to someone else or when we are involved in something urgent. But we can also learn to turn off the TV, put down the fashion magazine and give our undivided attention.

Let's re-examine our priorities and make time

for our children.

God gives me direction. Don't be afraid to give your child godly counsel based on Scripture and on the leading of the Holy Spirit.

Some Christian parents make the mistake of trying to live up to God's Word "to a point." If things don't work out immediately, they say, "Well, that didn't work. Let's try something else." What does that say to a child about the need to obey God? What does it say about the veracity of God's Word?

God always speaks life to me. Earlier, we were talking about forgiveness and how important it is not to "label" your child with a negative name or image. Here I want to take it a step further.

Jesus said, "The words that I speak unto you, they are spirit and they are life" (John 6:63). What did He mean?

Many parents tell their children all the things they'll never become, either out of fear or jealousy. Not only that, many times we are just plain nicer and more courteous to strangers in our place of business than we are to our own family at home.

We need to use our energy to speak *life* and to build up the faith of our young people. Consider what the writer of Proverbs had to say about the power of our words:

The tongue of the wise is health (12:18). Heaviness in the heart of a man maketh it stoop: but a good word maketh it glad (12:25).

A soft answer turneth away wrath: but grievous words stir up anger (15:1). A wholesome tongue is a tree of life (15:4).

God wants to use me. Many times, we're caught up in thinking and praying about what God wants to accomplish in our lives. But what about the lives of our children?

Paul knew that he would soon be leaving Timothy, his "son" in the Lord, when he wrote these instructions:

Neglect not the gift that is in thee (1 Tim. 4:14). Thou therefore, my son, be strong... study to shew thyself approved unto God (2 Tim. 2:1,15).

Our children ought to be taught that their youth doesn't exclude them from serving God in a worthwhile manner.

We can take these admonitions to heart and apply them in relation to our children. Rather than criticism and discouragement, let's plant in their hearts praise, kindness and a vision of what God can do through their lives.

Your Child's "Hearing Problem" and You

"OK," you may say, "I do my best to be a positive, upbeat, Christian parent. I don't put my child down or call him names. I encourage. I make myself available. He still doesn't seem to listen."

It's time I let the secret out: Every child has a

"hearing problem" when it comes to listening to parents.

You can stand toe-to-toe with your child and give a clear list of three things he must do before he can go out of the house. A half-hour later you'll find him sitting in front of the television with *nothing* done.

"Why didn't you do what I asked?" you demand.

He will nod feebly and say, "Oh, I didn't hear you."

We must recognize that we are engaged in spiritual warfare for our children. If we don't even train them to obey *our* voice, how can we ever expect them to hear and obey the voice of God?

How do you correct your child's "hearing problem"? The Bible has an answer. Proverbs 29:15 states,

> The rod and reproof give wisdom: but a child left to himself bringeth his mother to shame.

First of all, this instruction flies in the face of the prevailing lie that we should never spank our children. We've heard that countries like Sweden have *outlawed* spanking, and many Christians stomp up and down and say, "That's awful."

Many of us are guilty, however, of not correctly interpreting this scripture from Proverbs. I realized that, after quoting Solomon's instruction for years, I'd always had it backwards. Reading it in order, the way it's written, it says to use the rod first, then explain the reason for the discipline. If your child has that "spirit of deafness," the way to cast it out is with a rod!

How many of us take the time to explain ourselves to our children. Then when they don't obey, we explain ourselves again—a little louder this time. Then if they still don't obey, we explain ourselves at the top of our lungs! By this time, all the peace that is supposed to reign in our hearts and homes is destroyed.

If we use the rod when a child has disobeyed we're sure to get his attention. His mind will be open, let me assure you, and then we can give the godly instruction. As the verse in Proverbs points out, it's the rod first, then the imparting of reproof—or godly instruction. This is what leads a child to wisdom.

I've found that this formula really works, because I'm disciplining God's way and not my own.

The last portion of this verse says, "A child left to himself bringeth his mother to shame." When we allow our children to get away with things, we allow them to become self-serving, independent, stubborn and rebellious.

This is where we need to introduce that well-used—or misused—scripture, Proverbs 22:6:

> Train up a child in the way he should go: and when he is old, he will not depart from it.

To *train* means 1) to discipline, 2) to break and tame, and 3) to teach and form by practice. We've already discussed the order of godly discipline. What about taming and forming by practice?

My mother used to tell me that children need to be "broken," similar to the way you would break a colt. By this, we don't mean breaking the spirit, but breaking the will. The goal is to instill a respect for authority.

In James Dobson's film series, "Turn Your Heart Toward Home," he tells one story about a mother whose son wound up in jail. When the boy was three years old, he spit at her one day. Rather than spanking him, she spoke to him. He spit in her face again. She put him in his crib, and she walked out of his room. He spit at her back. "That was the moment I lost him," the woman said.

Friends, we must apply ourselves in the process of breaking the self-serving will that's in every child. We do not "provoke" our children to anger, which Paul warns against in Ephesians. But if we leave that self-will unbroken in a child, it will one day break him.

Lastly, we can teach and form our children by practice. This means living the example of a godly life in our homes. We can show our children what it means to live moral, clean, honest lives. If we don't hold up a standard for them, who will?

Let me put it bluntly: If we demand prayer in the public schools but don't pray as a family at home, we are nothing more than hypocrites. That may alarm or offend some, which I don't mean to do. I'm for getting prayer back into school. But why not start having a prayer time with your children before they leave the house in the morning?

As we order our children's lives, a funny thing happens. We find that we *re-order* our own lives. If we want to emphasize the importance of prayer and Bible reading to our children, we suddenly find that we must make room for this as a family in our own schedule. That may mean getting rid of some things that now take priority—like television, hobbies and extra trips to the shopping mall.

The prize is worth it! Just think. Not only will you build a whole new home-life centered in the Lord, but you are ordering your child's life and perhaps, through him, generations to come! And as we shape souls to serve God, we are giving to our Lord the gift of faithful servants in His glorious church.

Therefore, this is my prayer—and I hope it will be yours: Lord, teach me to communicate the goodness of Your life to my children, not my frustrations and anxieties. Help me to teach by *example* how great You are and how wonderful the Christian life is. Help me always to discipline as I ought and then to speak life. Raise up our children to be a mighty army of faith in the earth, Lord, to Your glory! Amen.

FIVE

Who Bakes Your Children's Bread?

So far, I've been addressing parents in general—both men and women. In this chapter, I want to speak directly to mothers. Now I don't want men to feel left out. I know that in this day, the father's role in raising godly children is finally being rediscovered—praise God!

But I know that women not only have it in their nature to birth children physically, but to "birth" ministries, gifts and talents as well. (And you fathers ought to read this chapter to know how to pray for your wives and their involvement in bringing up godly children.)

Mothers, I want you to consider with me Matthew 13:33. There we read,

Another parable spake he [Jesus] unto them;

The kingdom of heaven is like unto leaven, which a woman took, and hid in three measures of meal [that's seven and a half gallons], till the whole was leavened.

As I read that parable recently, it struck me that the faith, confidence, initiative and tenacity of a woman are being honored here by Jesus! He knows that it's in the nature of a woman to recognize something that has life or potential in it.

Not only that, once we have recognized the potential we want to nurture it and send it on to where there is no life at all. Because it's built into us to bring forth life, we women know that if we sow something, we are going to reap a harvest from it.

John 6 enlarges on that scripture. And it reveals more about the nature of a woman, especially in relation to the spiritual life of her children.

John tells us that Jesus was on a mountainside. He lifted His eyes and saw a great multitude. He knew these people were nearly famished with hunger, so He asked Philip to buy food for them. Philip must have gone cold. He knew they didn't have nearly enough money to feed the thousands of people who were present.

Then I read the words that stopped me. Andrew said, "There is a lad here..." (John 6:9).

You see, I am greatly concerned about the young people who are coming up today. No longer am I so concerned about my own ministry, but I'm turning around and looking at the generation that is on the horizon. They are anointed and called of God to a viable ministry—a whole new breed. And I'm concerned about who will "feed" them!

When Andrew pointed out the lad who was carrying the loaves and fishes, it made me think from a new perspective. When we are faced with difficulties, we always turn to those who are older and have experience. Why? Because we as adults tend to think that a young person *surely* can't know as much we do! Certainly they can't understand the complexities of today's issues, let alone be gifted enough to come up with the solution.

But Jesus willingly turned to a young man for the solution. Andrew said, "There is a lad here *which hath*...." The up-and-coming generation of young people *have something* that was given to them by God!

What did the boy have? Five barley loaves. In the Scriptures, five is the number that represents grace. Barley was the common grain. If people didn't have anything else, they had barley. Not only did the boy have barley, he had a spirit that was eager to give what was his own to be used by the Master.

God is going to use anyone who is willing. There is not an elite group, a special circle of people who are especially talented—He is going to use the common young man and woman!

How did the disciples respond when they saw the boy's simple provision? They asked, "But what are they among so many?" (John 6:9b).

They were saying, as we adults say, "Just look at the vastness of our problems. Look at the multitudes of unbelievers. Look at the need. Look at the horrors going on around us. Look at the darkness! What can a young person possibly do?"

As I was thinking these thoughts, the Spirit of God spoke to me and touched my heart with a further thought. He said, "There's more here. That boy didn't bake the bread. His *mother* did."

It's up to us to give our children the bread of life. It's up to Mama to bake the bread. We can provide spiritual sustenance for our children and not wait for our church or the school or the youth worker to do it. It's our responsibility to educate our children about the important things of life.

Sexuality

Too many of us cop out, for example, when it comes to the area of sexuality. We'll buy our children a book about sex and say, "Here, honey. Go read this." We rely on health or human sexuality courses in school. We complain that our churches need to be more "relevant," that youth workers need to teach morals and sexual ethics. Who says it's up to them? If it makes you uncomfortable to talk about such personal things, you can work on that. Because uncomfortable or not, the primary responsibility is ours!

Why am I emphasizing sexuality here? Because too many of us have become so "spiritual" that we can no longer be real.

Recently, on my television program, we discussed the subject of sex education and in-school clinics. The broadcast is done before a studio audience and we also take call-ins. During the time when I dialogue with people in the studio, I happened to be talking to an older woman, a pleasant-looking grandmother.

I asked her, "Did you talk to your children about their sexuality?"

She said, a little abruptly, "*No.*"

Where do you go from there? I asked, "Did your mother talk to you?"

Her shoulders sagged. This time she replied, with a good bit less starch, "No. And that's why I didn't talk to my children. I didn't know how."

During that same program, I was amazed and disappointed. I kept asking the same question and struck out every time. I talked with another grandmother, who told me her daughter ran away at sixteen and got married. I asked, "How did you prepare your daughter for marriage?"

She replied, as seriously as can be, "I told her to be a virgin."

Stunned, I asked, "Did she know what that meant?"

She replied, "I don't think so. And neither did I."

I realized in that moment why we have a promiscuous society—and it isn't just outside of the church. I've lived long enough and confronted enough to know. We're dealing with a very urgent subject.

Others I talked to said, "If I have a problem with one of my children, I just pray." Many said, "I talk to my pastor and he prays."

Folks, there is a time to pray and there is a time to take responsibility and do some talking.

There was one young lady on the program who introduced herself by saying that she was working to promote in-school clinics—a very unpopular position among Christians these days.

She said, "I'll have you know I'm a Christian. But I still believe we need the clinics in the school." Looking at those seated around her, she said, "*You* say we don't need those clinics to educate our children. You're depending on your church, and you're talking about educating your children.

"But what about all the children who don't have a church?" she continued. "Or those who have a church but don't have parents who will talk to them honestly. They know so little. And there is a plague of sexual diseases—including AIDS—in our world."

Her plea has made me think long and hard. Like so many, I've long held very conservative views about the role of the parent and the role of the school. But since that program, I've had to conclude that *parents* need to be educated as to their responsibility to give their children a godly perspective on all areas of life.

Not long ago, there was a big, full-page article in our newspaper on the subject of incest. I was dismayed to read the statistics and learn how prevalent this grievous sin is today.

As I drove to church that morning with Robin, I felt an inner nudge—an uncomfortable nudge, that is—to bring up the subject. I said, "Robin, have you ever heard the word 'incest'?"

"No," she shrugged.

"Do you have any idea what it means?" I asked.

Well, knowing that someday she might hear it from a friend, I took a deep breath and began to tell her what it meant. I hadn't gotten far before she interrupted me, with a look of horror and disgust, saying, "Mother, why on earth are you telling me this?"

"Because I don't want you to learn about life—even the bad things about life—by reading words on bathroom walls," I replied. "And I also want you to know that I'll answer any question if you'll ask me. We'll talk about anything, because I want you to hear it from me."

Now I've dwelt on the subject of sexuality, but, to me, we parents need to be at the forefront in presenting to our children all manner of knowledge, insofar as we can. But there is another area that we need to consider when it comes to the need to give spiritual "bread to our children."

Ministering to Their Souls

Sometimes we are quick to discipline, which we discussed in an earlier chapter. But I find that many of us give ministry or spiritual encouragement to others—and we neglect to minister to the souls of our own children.

Again, I was talking with Robin one day and, in a light mood, I asked, "What's the worst thing about being a minister's daughter?"

I thought—honestly I did—that she would say sweetly, "Oh, Mother, absolutely nothing."

Boy, was I wrong! I didn't have time to blink before she said, "No matter what I do, what I achieve or what I earn, the kids always tell me I got it because I was the pastor's daughter."

From that, I realized how much our children need for us to be sensitive to the challenges coming at them. On one hand, I do think that pastor's kids need a special type of ministry because of the fact that they live "in a goldfish bowl." Not only that, but if you have a church of five or 5,000, most of the folks are peering into that fish bowl and commenting on what's happening inside it!

But on the other hand, what young person today is not faced with challenges and temptations and pressures unheard of in history? Young people today have so much knowledge thrust upon them long before they know what to do with it, and less social controls to guide them into that wisdom.

Our children need to be ministered to.

Christian parents, do not make the mistake of thinking that church services are only for adults. Involve your children in your spiritual life. Take them with you as much as you possibly can. Let them be part of that world. Let them be there when the Spirit of God is poured out. Let them hear the prophecy.

Do your young people hear you talk about your spiritual ambitions and goals? Are they aware of the growth that's going on in you?

And how about this: Are you encouraging them to talk about the desires of their heart and what they think God might be calling them to do? Why is it that, when it comes to "serious" subjects like ministry, we parents can't believe that our children have a single, worthwhile thought in their heads or a dream in their hearts?

They do have both. And we can choose to be caught up in our own "adult" affairs, or we can nurture spiritual life and vision in our children.

Now let's return again to the mother of that lad with the loaves and fishes. I think I see something else about her.

She knew that she could not always be with him, that he had to go out on his own. So she made sure that, when he went out to face the day, he was *equipped* with that which would give him strength when he was tired and needed new energy. She saw to it that he was prepared.

This mother makes me think of the "virtuous woman" in Proverbs 31. "She gets up early...." I can't find anywhere a commission to be lazy or uninvolved. Throughout the Bible, I read about women who were on fire, hearing God and equipping their families.

Yes, the young lad's mama baked the loaves he gave to Jesus. And you and I need to be involved in baking the spiritual bread that nourishes our own.

Parents, I want to tell you something. Jesus is looking over multitudes who are in need. He is looking for someone to use to minister to countless hurting, broken, needy people. And when Jesus lays His hand on our children and takes hold of what we have imparted, He will say, "These young people have got something! I will take that bread, break it, bless it and use it to feed the world."

When we prepare our children and send them out, let's send them with *enough*—enough for themselves and enough to pass on to the hungry, hurting and broken. This young generation is a generation who will *need* more than enough bread in their baskets.

Recently, we were singing a chorus in our church, and these are some of the words:

It's beginning to rain, rain, rain!
Hear the voice of the Father,
"I'm going to pour my Spirit out
On your sons and your daughters."

As we sang it, the Lord said to me, "Are you *listening* to what you're singing? I'm going to pour My Spirit out on your young people. You have believed for revival in your generation, for a restoration of the gifts and ministries, for the salvation of multitudes.

"But this promise of revival among your sons and daughters is one that you've never taken hold of or held Me accountable for."

I was speechless—because it was the truth.

From that time I began to seek God on behalf of my daughter, wanting to know how I could "bake bread" to put in her basket. When my daughter has to face her world on her own, when she faces the challenges that lie ahead, I want her to have bread that is sufficient. Here I want to share with you what I have heard in prayer and in searching the Scriptures for an answer.

I believe God wants us to tell our children that God's hand is upon them—that they are called by Him.

When I shared this with a friend, she challenged me and said, "How could you possibly tell your daughter she's got a call of God?"

And I said, "Because God told me! He didn't say what *kind* of call—it's up to Him to tell her specifically. But I'm not going to wait until she's hanging over hell by a hair, half-dead in a car wreck, and hope that she will wake up and say, 'Oh Lord, save me because I know I'm supposed to serve You. Just spare my life and I'll do it.' "

I don't want to wait until my child has fallen in a pigsty or tasted all the "pleasures" of Egypt for a season to tell her she is marked for God—do you? Moses' mama did such a good job of marking her son that if Egypt had ever really gotten hold of him it would have spit him out!

Some of us, unfortunately, spend too much time rebuking the devil in our prayers for our children. You can rebuke him once, believe it's done, then spend the rest of your time building up your child! Your words can give life, purpose, direction— and they can impart the love of God.

Mothers, millions are walking the roads of this life hungry, unloved, lost and alone. You are the one who can bake bread for your son or daughter.

Then, in God's timing, you will be blessed to watch Him lay His hand on your child's shoulder and say, "Let Me see what you have in your basket...."

SIX

A Generation That Will

We've focused on the spiritual battle for our own families. Before we look at the unusual challenge that faces our children, I think it's important that we understand what is happening on a broader scale.

Today a spiritual war is raging for the mind of every man, woman and child. What are the weapons used against us? Every high thought that exalts itself against the knowledge of the one true God (2 Cor. 10:5). The prize of this warfare? Our eternal souls.

The weapons formed against us have many names: secular humanism, communism, Eastern religions, even *liberal* Christianity. It's interesting, though, that when evil tries to lull the human spirit to sleep, the Spirit of God is stirring His people to arms.

Consider, for example, an article about the church in Russia that appeared in the San Francisco *Tribune*. I think it's important enough to reproduce at length:

TELEVISION SHOW FINDS SOVIETS CANNOT BUY RELIGION

NEW YORK (AP)—In the early days of the Soviet Union its leader, Lenin, said its system was disturbing the "fad" of religion and liberating the worker from it. But after 65 years of communist rule in an officially atheistic nation, the workers refuse to be "liberated" from the faith, says the narrator of an extraordinary NBC television documentary exploring religious life in the USSR.

"Religion remains a daily fact of life in the Soviet Union and is now displaying signs of a greater strength and growth than ever before" (the narrator declared).

..."Religion is indeed alive and thriving in the USSR," says the executive producer to the NBC news program. "That's the story we've come back to tell."

But they are restricted—there is not religious freedom as you and I know it. Nevertheless, they are sincere and hungry enough to reach for God.

The article goes on to relate these accounts:

At the Moscow seminary a second-year student tells how he grew up in a non-religious family but reached a point where he began to ponder the meaning of life. When he first visited a church at the age of fifteen, he said he was intrigued and yet had no idea what was going on. He then began to read and search for answers.

A woman feeding pigeons in a public park was heard singing an old Russian folk song: "Please do not forsake us. Have mercy. The kingdom of God we accept and love." This, if overheard by the police, would mean years in prison.

A minister spoke openly of faith and a "Law Giver who is higher than the constricted views of materialism—a God who must be served."

The archbishop of the Russian Orthodox Church was quoted as saying, "Up to sixty percent of the crowded Sunday meetings are young people between the ages of twenty and thirty... young adults searching for God."

It thrilled me to read this article. Even though the USSR in policy is an atheistic country and has tried to stamp out the knowledge of God for more than sixty-five years, a new generation that wants to serve God is rising up!

Obviously, this indicates that there have been parents who have remained faithful to keep God's Word alive despite threats and official repression. Like the mother and father of Moses, these men and women have not feared the wrath of the government, have not been afraid to suffer if need be in order to pass on their faith to their children.

Second, a climate of faith in closed countries

like Russia says to me that the apostle Paul was correct when he wrote in Romans 8:39 that "[nothing] in all creation will be able to separate us from the love of God that is in Christ Jesus our Lord" (NIV).

This verse, and the testimony of faithfulness of these Christian parents in Russia, give me great hope as I pray for the spiritual growth of our young people in America.

Third, I realize that, even when there is a generation that *won't* worship God, like those who spawned the Bolshevik Revolution, God is at work to raise up a generation that will.

When the Word of God Is Found

What is happening in the Soviet Union and in other nations today reminds me of the days of Josiah, who was king of Judah at a time of great unbelief. Now the three kings who preceded Josiah present an interesting picture.

Hezekiah was king at the time of the prophet Isaiah and was a much-respected and godly man. His son Manasseh, however, was another story! Not only did Manasseh build pagan shrines in the Lord's temple in Jerusalem, he allowed both male and female prostitutes to practice their trade there. He also practiced sorcery, communicated with evil spirits and even sacrificed his own son by fire to a demon god. During his rule, he led all of Judah into sin against the Lord. (See 2 Kings 21.)

Manasseh's son, Amon, was just as wicked.

The Bible says,

> He did evil in the eyes of the Lord, as his father Manasseh had done....He forsook the Lord (2 Kings 21:20,22, NIV).

Perhaps because he was so evil and out of control he was assassinated by his own officials right in his palace.

Look at the startling contrast in the life of Josiah. We read in 2 Kings 22 that he sent his secretary to Hilkiah, the high priest. Josiah ordered that the temple treasuries be broken open and the money be used to hire workmen and buy supplies to restore the temple, which his father and grandfather had allowed to fall to ruin. The secretary discovered that, not only was Hilkiah eager to obey the king, he had a surprise of his own.

Hilkiah greeted the secretary with these urgent words: "I have found the Book of the Law in the temple of the Lord" (vs. 8, NIV). Apparently, the priests had concealed a scroll with the books of Moses to prevent the complete destruction of God's Word by the previous evil kings. Now, from some secret corner, God brought it to light again!

When the secretary carried the scroll to Josiah, the king ordered it read at once. What we see next is perhaps one of the greatest acts of repentance in all history. You can feel the horror in Josiah's heart as he hears God's Word and compares it to the evil of his forefathers. In verse 11 we read, "When the king heard the words of the Book of the Law, he tore his robes.''

Immediately, Josiah renewed the covenant with God. He ordered the destruction of all pagan shrines and the death of those priests who had turned from the Lord to serve false gods. The most telling statement comes at the very end of this marvelous story:

> Neither before nor after Josiah was there a king like him who turned to the Lord as he did—with all his heart and with all his soul and with all his strength in accordance with the Law of Moses (2 Kings 23:25, NIV).

Some of the parallels between Josiah's day and our own are alarming—and at the same time challenging.

Good News—and a Warning

Today, children are being sacrificed on the demonic altars of lust, self-interest, child pornography and abortion. As we said earlier, there seems to be an all-out war against children! Our leaders are falling into disrepute and the church is being shaken. Not only that but there is an attempt to ''hide'' the Word of God. It has been taken out of our classrooms. It is being distorted by liberal seminaries. A few people in high places in our society seem determined to replace the redemptive power of the Bible with the lie of secular humanism.

Someone is trying to wipe out all knowledge

of God.

But I see another side, too. Good news!

When Josiah rediscovered the Word of the Lord, he understood its meaning for his generation. He spoke to the people and said, "We haven't kept God's Word and great wrath will be poured on us."

Even so, today, there is a rallying cry within the church. Armies of God's people are banding together to tear down the strongholds of abortion and lenient laws that condone the pornography that victimizes women and our young. Christians are standing against the tide of humanism that wants to hide the Word of God and *dehumanize* us.

And yet there is a frightening *other* side to what is happening. While we Christians are demanding public morality, we are slipping in our own private morality. For too long we've been a generation of church-going folk whose philosophy has been: "Just about anything is OK to do, as long as I don't hurt anybody. After all, everybody's doing it"— whatever *it* happens to be.

Among Christians, for example, the divorce rate is cresting like a wave. The world can marry, divorce, remarry and divorce again, but you and I can't live that way.

Now before this starts to sound like finger-pointing, let me hasten to say that I agree with what Billy Graham once said on the subject of divorce. He said, in essence, "If you've sinned in the area of divorce, admit it. Tell God, ask His forgiveness, be washed in the blood of Jesus, arise and sin no more. Then serve God with all your heart, mind and strength." Which is exactly what Josiah did.

But let's emphasize getting back to the Bible. Instead of condoning sin under the guise of Christian "sympathy," let's declare the truth: It's better not to sin in the first place. Let's proclaim that we must run from sin and avoid it at all costs.

Sin cripples us and the work of the Holy Spirit in our lives. It is in truth and purity and obeying the unmixed Word of God that His power is let loose in us.

How does this relate to marking your children for God?

One of the most crucial ways in which we shape our children is in the attitude we take toward *sin*. Let me ask you some questions. Do you hate divorce the way the Bible says God hates it? Do you hate the fact that millions of unborn babies are being aborted in our country—hundreds of them this very moment as you read? Or are you noncommital and lukewarm about these sins that grieve God's heart?

Before you think, "Well, abortion is an issue I don't have to deal with," let me tell you a story.

A friend who is a minister recently told me about a Christian couple in his church who came to him for help with a serious problem. Their unwed daughter was pregnant. Since the girl did not want to keep the child, and the parents did not want to raise it, my friend advised that they contact one of the agencies that minister to unwed mothers. They could help through the pregnancy and also adopt out the child after its birth.

One weekend, he noticed that the family was not in church. When they returned, the parents told him they had taken their daughter out of town so she could have an abortion.

The minister told me that, following this action, he watched as the family slowly and pathetically dissolved. The daughter and the other children dropped out of church and fell away from the Lord. Gradually, the family was destroyed.

Why? The parents had taken the attitude, "Of course, we can say abortion is wrong—but this time it's *our* daughter who's pregnant. So the rules of God don't apply." What they did was to teach their children that God's Word is not as important as personal convenience.

But before you shake your head knowingly— don't we do the same at times? Think of the times when a ball game or a trip to the beach has been more important than being in church on Sunday. Think of the times we've cheated on our tithes or begrudged an offering in order to get new drapes or golf clubs or to have a little extra to spend on vacation.

Earlier we talked about marking our children by example and commitment. Now we are talking about something far more important. *When the Word of God is found, are we going to obey it?*

There is a realm of God that we need to move into, and we only do this by obedience to His Word. In Numbers 14:22-23 we read,

> Because all those men have seen my glory and my miracles...and have not hearkened to my voice; surely they shall not see the land which I sware unto their fathers, neither shall any of them that provoked me see it.

Yet we immediately find hope. In the next verse, we read,

> But my servant Caleb, because he had another spirit with him, and hath followed me fully, him will I bring into the land whereinto he went, *and his seed shall possess it* (italics mine).

The same incredible promise was not given to others of Caleb's generation. They were a people who were always bargaining with the Lord or else turning away from Him. When the battle came and it was time to take a stand for the Lord, they refused to budge.

Friends, what kind of example are we setting when it comes to moral issues? Are we, like Josiah, willing to repent for the deeds of preceding generations of Christians who had a lackadaisical response to God's Word? A third to half of our unborn children are being annihilated in a silent holocaust—and this is just one sin against the human race and against God. Are we still afraid to rock the boat and lose social acceptability, or do we demonstrate for our children a healthy fear of the Lord?

Speaking of the children of those disobedient Israelites, God said in Numbers 14,

> ...them will I bring in, and they shall know the land which ye have despised. But as for you, your carcasses, they shall fall in this wilderness (vv. 31,32).

These are not pleasant words to point out to you. But they happen to be the Word of God to us today.

There is a generation that will enter into God's inheritance. They are here among us—in our homes and sitting in our Sunday school rooms! How do I know this?

We hear God speaking about this generation in a prophetic passage from the Psalms:

> That the children to come might know them, *even the children which should be born*; who should arise and declare them [God's Word] to their children: that they might set their hope in God, and not forget the works of God, but keep his commandments (Ps. 78:6,7, italics mine).

Furthermore, God says through David,

> Who shall ascend into the hill of the Lord? or who shall stand in His holy place? He that hath clean hands and a pure heart; who hath

not lifted up his soul unto vanity, nor sworn deceitfully. He shall receive the blessing from the Lord, and righteousness from the God of His salvation. This is the generation of them that seek him, that seek thy face... (Ps. 24:3-6).

This is happening now—today! Young men and women from Russia to the streets of America are seeking God and His salvation. I believe that our teenagers, our young men and women, are the generation that will repossess this land for God. And they can enter the promises of God with us, their parents, or without us. That choice is up to us.

Friends, though it's been tough for me to speak as plainly as I have in this chapter, I believe that God has better things in mind for *our* generation, too. I believe we can receive the blessing of God along with our children. But that will depend on our catching God's vision for our young people—a generation who will.

For when we get our lives straight according to the Word of God, then begin to invest our energies and moral commitment into our children—well, we are on the brink of a revival in America.

A day is about to dawn in which the church will be restored. Even now the Word of God is being rediscovered. Let's search His Word carefully, for in it we will see the truth about the generation that is being restored. For they will reveal His glory in all the earth!

SEVEN

Restoration of Our Children

*T*hroughout this book, we've used terms like "warfare" and "fighting the fight of faith" as they apply to marking our children for God. Anyone who has had children knows these terms apply, and I wouldn't want to mislead anyone by making them think being a godly parent is easy.

But I'd be misleading you if I didn't declare that a new day is dawning. I see a new, godly family on the horizon!

How do I know that?

I have learned to read "the signs of the times." We are entering one of the most awesome periods in the history of mankind. Let me share a brief overview with you.

His Glory Is Rising Upon Us

Do you ever pray, "Lord, just send Your glory—fill the whole earth with it!"

Have I got good news for you! Isaiah 6:3 says,

The whole earth *is* full of his glory (italics mine).

Friends, the earth is still full of the glory of the Lord. Full and getting fuller all the time. Revival waves are beginning to crash on the shores of our day.

Early in this century, a great revival swept out from Wales to Britain to Azusa Street in California. Wave upon wave of God's glory crashed into the church! On it went into the Middle East and China—around the world. Pentecost hit and was in full swing by 1908.

Forty years later, in 1948, something unusual happened. On May 14 of that year, the nation of Israel came into being overnight—as if by a miracle. The rebirth of that ancient land was more than a political incident. Something was breaking loose in the spiritual realm.

If you were to ask some of our greatest Christian leaders today when their ministry took off, they would quickly say, "In 1948!" The Latter Rain movement began; tent meetings and revival centers sprang up; independent churches opened their doors. Billy Graham, Oral Roberts, Jack Coe, William Branham, Demos Shakarian, Daisy and

T.L. Osborn, Rex Humbard, Kathryn Kuhlman—all these leaders emerged and mark the real explosion of their ministries from the late 1940s.

It's also interesting to me that in 1948, the National Council of Churches was formed and apartheid became law in South Africa—movements running counter to the restoration of truth and freedom.

But the waves that began in 1948 kept on splashing on into the 1960s. God sent renewal, revival. He poured out His Spirit on the Catholics, Presbyterians, Amish, Mennonites, Methodists, Baptists. We called it the "charismatic renewal." It hit everyone!

Now as we look at the pattern, at the rhythm of revival, we have to ask: When can we expect the next big waves to hit the shore?

The answer is: We are due—maybe overdue—for another great revival!

Let me say quickly that there are some today who insist that Jesus must return in 1988. They determine that by conjecture from Jesus' prophecies in Matthew 24 about the end times. There He indicated that Israel would be drawn together as a nation after a great time of dispersal. Then He promised that the generation that witnessed this event "shall not pass till all these things be fulfilled" (Matt. 24:34).

I have to confess that, while I would love to see Jesus return today, I think it's unwise to set dates for the event. Many have tried. Jesus Himself said,

"But of that date and hour knoweth no man...but my Father only" (v. 36).

Nonetheless, Jesus told us over and over to "watch." And He told us to be wise by reading "the signs of the times."

Friends, I say to you that all the events from the restoration of Israel in 1948 up until now have been like small waves, building in frequency and power.

If you've ever been to the ocean and watched surfers, they catch smaller waves, all the while watching the horizon for that big wave to hit. It's like that with revival. You see a stirring. The untrained eye wouldn't notice—but the person who is trained knows what's coming. Revival!

Now when the revival of the 1500s hit—the one we call the Reformation—God opened to us a knowledge of His Word. In the revival of the 1800s, we received the message of holiness, that God meant for us to be a called-out, separate and sanctified people. In the early 1900s, the miraculous power of the Holy Spirit was restored in our lives, not just to perform miracles but to heal us inwardly and make the character of Christ available to us.

Over and over the church has been hit by the Spirit's life-giving water and the blazing, intense light of His presence. And do you know what water and heat do when they mix together—they create steam. And steam removes spots and irons out wrinkles!

Friends, God is getting the spots and wrinkles out of the wedding garment of His bride. Yes, the next revival that is about to come crashing in upon us is going to be big. You see, we are coming into the restoration of all things.

A New Generation

Among other things, I believe that *this* move of God's Spirit is bringing the restoration of godly families—and children who really know the Lord.

In Joel 2, the Lord spoke through His servant to tell about a time when His Spirit would fall as rain upon the earth. He gave us this marvelous promise:

> And it shall come to pass afterward, that I will pour out my spirit on all flesh; *and your sons and your daughters shall prophesy*, your old men shall dream dreams, your *young men shall see visions* (v. 28, italics mine).

These are some of the signs of the coming restoration of God's Spirit to His church. We can expect that our children will move into the things of God. And we can take part in their preparation!

We do that by overthrowing our fear of men and rebellious attitudes. We do that by becoming parents in the Lord. We overthrow the unbelieving attitude that assumes our children will be cold toward God and will follow the crowd into drugs and illicit sex. We refuse to accept as normal that, once a child becomes a teenager, he can shut himself away in his room and forsake the life of the family.

Prepare your children today for the role God has for them in this exciting and crucial hour. Allow them to be taught about spiritual things—the gifts of the Spirit, the ministries. Speak words of encouragement, telling them that God definitely has a place for them in His service. Tell them to listen for His voice, for as surely as He called young Samuel, God wants to speak to the heart of your child.

This is not to play up our children and take away from all that God has been doing in *our* generation. Quite the opposite. When Joel prophesied and said, "Your old men will dream dreams," the Spirit spoke to my heart. He said, "It is because the old men dream dreams and set an example for the younger generation that the young men learn to expect visions!"

You see, as our young people are exposed to the things of God, they begin to perceive the ways the Lord wants to speak to them. They learn how it is you hear His voice, what it means to obey—and also the rewards that come from following the Spirit!

One of the new things that I see happening among our young people is a "rediscovery" of the true Word of God, just as young King Josiah discovered it.

In the early part of our century, the church was infected with a creeping pessimism. This came in large part because of the theory of evolution and because of two devastating world wars. On one hand there was a demoralization of Christians. But on the other hand, there was a swing toward isolation. During that time, the doctrine of the "rapture" seemed to offer the most hope and quick release from this world. And so we Christians abandoned our place in politics, government, education and other "worldly" pursuits.

But I believe that our young people will again "dust off the Book," as Josiah did, and see what it really says. For we are told that the Word of God must go forth into the whole world and *then* shall the end come. God has given us the heathen as our inheritance. Our mandate is to conquer!

So our young people are destined to become a mighty army for the Lord, once they become involved in His vision for the restoration of the church.

We must not take this call lightly. Numbers 14:31 tells of a generation of parents who doubted the inheritance promised to their children:

> But your little ones, *whom you said would be victims*, I will bring in, and they shall know the land which you have despised (NKJV, italics mine).

Have we doubted our children's inheritance in God's kingdom? Have we been afraid that the way is too narrow and too straight for them to follow?

They are going to make it in fine style! They are

going to possess the land. The proper raising of our children will not be futile.

It is with joy and excitement that I exhort you: Do not be timid about marking your children for God. The world isn't the least bit timid about trying to put its evil mark on them.

Start to lay hands on them and pray. Continue to pray for them and *with* them all through their teenage years. Assure your children that they are called of God, chosen and anointed.

Church, the time is upon us for the restoration of biblical patterns in our homes and families. It is time to be bold in marking our children for the Master's use.

For when we give ourselves and our children to Him, we find that His kingdom moves into our daily lives, changing everything about us.

Then, I believe, we will see the great restoration of all things!

EPILOGUE

A Word of Hope
For the Long Road

*J*ust at the time I was working on this book, I was speaking at a very large convention. There a remarkable thing happened.

The hall was full. In fact, people were sitting on the floor and lining the back wall. I gave the message I believe the Lord wanted me to give that day, but when I'd finished, I noticed that three or four minutes were left in the session. Casually, I remarked about the great things I see ahead for our children and the fact that Christian parents can have the blessing of marking their children for God.

At the close of the session I was mobbed! A few people commented on my first address, but all the rest were excited about what had come in the last few minutes. They were all eager for some word of encouragement about their children.

One woman touched me most deeply.

She was a mother with a son in his forties. "He's away from the Lord," she told me, and I could hear her voice choking as she said those words. "I've been praying for him for such a long time. What do you think I should do, Anne?"

"Tell him that he belongs to God," I told her. "Tell him he belongs to God. A son or daughter can turn you off and turn away. But I know one thing.

"In the night hours, when they wake up and lie there in the dark, your words will come back. And the Holy Spirit will use those words to open his spirit and go deep. There is nothing that can penetrate a child's heart like the words of his mama or daddy."

She seized my hands, her face now flooded with a warm smile. "Thank you, Anne. I needed those words, because I've needed hope."

I know this woman is not alone. There are thousands of parents out there who hope with all their hearts that their children will become men and women of faith.

My comfort, and yours, lies in the fact that it is never too early to mark our children for God. And, praise God, it is never too late!

OTHER PUBLICATIONS
OF INTEREST FROM
CREATION HOUSE

The Emerging Christian Woman
by Anne Gimenez

Women are on the move. They are shaking off many years of silence and passivity. Inspired by the Spirit, they are assuming their proper roles of leadership in the body of Christ. Anne believes Christ is calling Christian women to take a lead in bringing new life, healing and unity to the church. $4.95

Help! I'm a Pastor's Wife
edited by Michele Buckingham

Thirty women, some famous, some not-so-famous, open their hearts with amazing frankness and tell of their heartaches and joys, their defeats and victories as wives of modern pastors and teachers. They write from four perspectives: wife, mother, woman and minister. $9.95